THE GOOD BACTERIA

THE
GOOD
BACTERIA

SHARON
THESEN

ANANSI

Published in 2006 by
House of Anansi Press Inc.
110 Spadina Avenue, Suite 801
Toronto, ON, M5V 2K4
Tel. 416-363-4343
Fax 416-363-1017
www.anansi.ca

Distributed in Canada by
HarperCollins Canada Ltd.
1995 Markham Road
Scarborough, ON, M1B 5M8
Toll free tel. 1-800-387-0117

Distributed in the United States by
Publishers Group West
1700 Fourth Street
Berkeley, CA 94710
Toll free tel. 1-800-788-3123

10 09 08 07 06   1 2 3 4 5

LIBRARY AND ARCHIVES CANADA CATALOGUING IN PUBLICATION DATA
Thesen, Sharon, 1946–
The good bacteria : poems / Sharon Thesen.

ISBN 0-88784-746-3

I. Title.
PS8589.H433G65 2006   C811'.54   C2005-907352-7

LIBRARY OF CONGRESS CONTROL NUMBER: 2006920152

*We acknowledge for their financial support of our publishing program
the Canada Council for the Arts, the Ontario Arts Council, and the Government of
Canada through the Book Publishing Industry Development Program (BPIDP).*

Printed and bound in Canada

He who has kissed
a leaf

need look no further—
I ascend

through
a canopy of leaves

and at the same time
I descend

for I do nothing
unusual—

I ride in my car
I think about

prehistoric caves

—W.C. WILLIAMS, *SPRING AND ALL, 1923*

CONTENTS

THE GOOD BACTERIA

1.

They had a view of the twinkling city as they ate.
Car lights were a ribbon along the shape of the bridge.
No one was there; they were all ghosts in coats.

No more bloody ghazals! one ghost shouted to another.
In the morning they ate again, and took their penicillin pills.
The penicillin killed the good bacteria as well as the bad.

It killed all the bacteria, good and bad, like death or God.
Though death, being a matter of bacteria, is also life.
It was easier to walk to Kamloops.

He lugged his own laptop; it was easier that way.
On his lap sat the known universe.
When he sat down, the known universe sat on his lap.

He could see anything that way on the way to Kamloops.
A known ghost. The trees burned all the way to the sky.
His stomach burned when he took the penicillin.

2.

She pressed upon the part of her mind
that was titanium, Queen of the Fairies.

Lighter than air almost she was wringing salt
out where she'd wept into her hair.

Perched on a pear
leaf leaning out to see
insect heraldry. And to call
for a change in government.

With subtle blush and translucent
garments at 3:00 a.m. calling the cat away
from mouse ribs lest coyotes
with licked chops sneak up and pounce

like the government upon the night-shift
poor and tired.

3.

A white lake gull grabbed a breeze.
Me and my sister were lying on the rocky beach.

A duck went swimming by, really hauling.
Seeing my sister he married her and she married him.
Down they went to an underwater house
whose chimney comes out where
the smoke bush grows.

Beside the smoke bush the electricity inspector
peers at a gauge on the house wall and writes
in his book.

My sister comes up for air and shakes herself
somewhat dry although her rump — so quick
to propel her downward to her happy home —
leaves a damp imprint on the car seat.

We poke at buttons on the dash until we get
some music we like. Another button and
the windows go down. Hand out, fingers
spread plying the warm currents of Peachland.

4·

As if we loved not only each other
but the weather we were happy
when the hummingbirds came
with suggestive beaks to the nectar-laden
honeysuckle and hovered shimmering like
someone wrote, *a winged mouse*. It was in
a not-nice book, especially the part
where the blameless woman's heart was broken.

They'd met for the first time at a clinic
with a terrible insect bite that would not go down.

After that they were inseparable. The book —
a novel — was set in the Arizona desert where no
apparent difference obtained between
life and death, taxidermy came up often
as a metaphor or a simile, a smile

often lurking on its countenance.

5.

A woman with the face of a sheepdog
or a sheepdog with the face of a woman
was sitting beside the driver—a young
Caucasian male—of a black F150 pickup truck
speeding south on South Ridge Drive.

Anubis, anubis, what a heck of a proboscis!

Later, a heart-rending bawling as of a goat
led to the slaughter echoed among the monster houses.

6.

Small round islands crammed with tall trees,
toupees of underwater giants. On balder crowns
eagles rest hooded and quiet, hangmen
at lunchtime.

Always losing wives. They disappear through
pinholes in the bottom of the ocean. They belong
to the goose world. Honking and hollering,
their divine soft breasts and missing children
sitting on a seat on an airplane. All the crying
and the carrying on, agencies like you wouldn't
believe, all helpless. Infinite worlds.

7.

In this life it has not been given me
to see that many bears.

One by the Hope-Princeton Highway.
One by the road up near Masset.
Another when a kid in Banff
where they wandered among the cars.

One on a hillside near some horses grazing
but it could have been a scarecrow,
dark silhouette constructed of plywood
and erected in a bad mood
to discourage swans & other
beautiful things from landing and settling
with wide wings from elsewhere.

8.

I saw him coming down the street in the sunshine
eating an apple he'd bought at the grocery store.
The sea, the sea
glinted and humped behind him
devoid of any but anchored boats

his own waited in a tree
and had the face of a woman
he'd married once in a dream—

thereafter she carried him
on her back until the dream ended.

An orange popsicle was softening
in the grocery bag. While he sat in the café
among other songless birds
it melted, then liquefied, then vanished.

9.

And still the government remained the same
or worse. And what was frozen resumed.

And others fainted and fell to the ground.
Thinking themselves joined to the ineffable
with rubber bands and with foreknowledge,
so they could faint and fall, faint and fall
all day if they wanted.

Still the traffic twinkled on the bridge
and the lights of the dwellings along the shore
and higher up in the mountains twinkled
also as soon as night fell and all night
until morning the measure of those who forgot to turn out
their front porch light would be taken
by the electricity inspector.

Dials and gauges tremble with information,
the smoke bush sends out a new red shoot.

Quickly the sun rises like a big monster.
The moon is vanquished unlike ignorance
unlike getting it all wrong unlike we did it ourselves.

10.

Across the hills and valleys
hurrying as if excited to have
found a dollar bill.

They had something to tell.
They concealed redness.

They humped over and between.
They were infinite in number
leading up the last one.

Circlets of blossom crown sleek heads
in the Olympic-size pool which quickly
are gone. The surface is silent.

Then erupts with smiles. Ducks
quack in the current of the stream
so bright they look painted.

On a treetop above, an eagle
devours a dead crow and black feathers
are drifting down.

The dead crow's best friend sobs nearby.
Everything moving and dropping.

11.

Under the scabbard and cover of night
Entrances islanded.
Potholders suspended from a daisy.

Complicated crosses with crooks.
And knots. Knotted and beguiled.
A swag of painted cherries like wounds lined up.

Circlets of roses, circlets of roses with ribbons.
Picture of three fishing boats two tall one small
Between them, their reflections waver.

Sea Grove, Potatoes, Swagman appear
To be the names painted on them from afar.
You can just hear the seagulls screeching in the dawn.

The subject is elusive, like Artemis.
In those woods she shines but not here
In the house where all is pinkish.

Enter a real guy in a pleated skirt with a sword
Sunk in a scabbard, ten oxen
Couldn't drag him away from fighting.

Inside his myth he's very busy too.
Polishing his scabbard with Silvo, staunching
His cuts and abrasions he goes through tubes of Polysporin.

12.

There was a lot of waiting along the road.
Her brother sat in a truck all day waiting like this.
He saw some smoke then some helicopters
And airplanes casting orange smoke.

It was lunchtime just before the sawdust pile
Ignited from within. It was just like a movie
Or a corpse. Many corpses had been found
Under cars and on the road and in the market.

Pale-winged hawks hunted mice at the top.
They cast wide circles.
Even the dog looked like a cat at a mousehole
Digging and digging and staring stock still.

The mice and the fires had a field day.
Me and my brother walked for a while
On the road that had no cars, that stayed
Between pines and tall white plants and purple ones.

Already we could hear the sound of the traffic.
Traffic and houses made of wood with maple cabinets,
An island kitchen, and killer ensuite.
In the dream we had, a mountain fell down.

I was calling the name of my son.

A HOLY EXPERIMENT

1. Jerry Geiger was friend of Frances Bolderleff's when she lived in Woodward, Pennsylvania, many years ago.

2. In worn-out chairs, we sat in his kitchen.

3. For this ailment, for that, he had a cure.

4. We were staying at an old, old inn.

5. Expressways and turnpikes, off-ramps, antacid vapour lights.

1.

One night, he had her look at the sky through his telescope.
"That's the MOON?" Frances said. It was sometime in the mid- to
    late fifties, "La Motz" was
one of her noms de plume.

After the funeral & the small
gathering afterward at the house, Jerry talked
about the massive heavy presses made of ancient
wood and stone that every autumn
were used to press the apple cider.

The icy cold cider lay in tanks in the earth. Any
sort of jar with a lid stored it —
pickle jars, mayonnaise jars. While visiting Jerry
the next day we had a glass or two each.

Up in the watchtower where he once
kept his telescope we ascended narrow stairs,
looked out as if we were Frances that night,
came back down the steep stairway with serious faces,
a wooden stairway more like a ladder.

Not far, over some mountains, the current of the Susquehanna River
pouring, the beautiful word "Susquehanna" new to my tongue.

We said goodbye beside the rental car in the rain. Along the path,
fierce little mottled apples strewn by the wind and at the cemetery
the ashes of Frances beneath a fresh pile of dirt in the family
plot, a dozen granite headstones all saying MOTZ.

2.

Rows and jars of homemade reddish-brown &
dark green medicines, gathered from the
plush land at the end of the road. The world was different
and quite what I guess I would call "American."

He had asked Frances to look at the moon through his telescope.
The night must have been clear and black, the moon
bright and full. What did she see: a bunch of
shadows, crags and valleys, craters full of
darkness. Were they lovers, we were dying to ask. Whatever,
he had a Doctorate in the Metaphysics of Spirals.

That shut us up for a while.

He must have brought her over from Woodward
in his car to view the moon. She had already named him
president of her five-book publishing company,
where every cent poured, to which she sacrificed
the rent and went for years without a decent hairbrush.

3.

He could have been a soldier
in the last years of the war
or come of age around the time I was born.

Maybe this has to do with the weirdness
and warp of time, the spiralling, going nowhere.
One is neither here nor there
and doesn't know what to say.

One sits in the perished chair and listens.
Like a bending of the rain the thought of William Penn,
said to have been fair and wise
which is why the Indians trusted him.
Attractive, idealistic, clear-eyed—
this charisma led them all to a *holy experiment.*

Science magazines in stacks
on the kitchen table, radio antennas
at several different angles conspire in the ether.

4.

What if something supernatural happened?
Floors sloped, ornate would be the preferred
décor of such a place, visited by tourists,
mourners, certain parties of folks.

The rain fell heavily on the Susquehanna
and on the Indians and the Germans
in their graves, if they had them
and didn't just die in the woods with an antique
rifle or a hatchet in their hands.

And almost like those dead I slept
and forgot my tickets and passport

So I had to return
to the little house
and ask to use the phone
which ruins everything
since you've said goodbye, you're
in the past, and now
you're back.

They dial for you if you can't find your glasses
right away. And when you leave for the second time
let's all hope it will be the last.

5.

The Susquehanna would reveal
what lay around the bend in the beauty and the silence—
the silence of nature, not silent at all.

In her night-time I wandered afresh with
the map obscure by my side,
a rough map the size of a place-mat. So many roads,
so little time! I tore along in the purple Galanta
looking for turnoffs, slowed on village streets, places
crowded close to the road like Aaronsburg,
Jerry's place not far from there where hills
and woods began.

Farmland all around, farms out of a story-
book hugely romanticized. Mennonite,
Amish, or just plain Yanks wearing rain jackets and
opening doors. Any autumn afternoon was sepia-toned
and frightened, like a commercial for insurance.

Long ago of course this was all moot or a moat.
Motz built Woodward & Frances who like a deity
had many names and situations sacred to her ups and downs

returned to be a Motz in the cemetery across the road
from her parlour, her library.

RELATIVE TO HISTORY

Hey I Think That's Me

Let's say it was 1971. *The Edge of Night* was on TV.
It was a Thursday afternoon in February, I remember the living room
and the cars going by out the window.

The kitchen was tidy if not exactly spanking clean. I'd
probably read a Lew Welch poem and hung out diapers.
The wall phone would ring twice any minute.

A shotgun stood in the corner of the back room.
Raccoons, FBI, snakes, intruders—
you never knew.

Quietly the days went by like this,
in the house with the baby, poetry, washing my hair
and ironing a blouse to wear to the dentist. The Novocaine
hit my veins, I thought I'd pass out, maybe die.

Why were we living like this? The stupid shotgun,
pretense of what?—the moose-meat roast
when the Minskys came over for dinner. Let's just say
it wasn't all my idea, nor was I particularly enjoying myself.

An allegiance to a certain way of being
seemed necessary, to be tough-minded with wire eyeglasses,
enraged and sad but also handsome and

Opportunistic. We went to the door with glee
knowing someone American & good-looking was there
with books and hashish and news about the concerts and riots.

Tinseltown

Busy and in the upper registers
        rain incessant in the night
                teems from sky to earth

where SkyTrain also
        creaks and zooms
                irrespective of us, who will drive

thank you very much
        to Tinseltown.

It won't be far
        & we'll park
                underneath the gates of Chinatown

& watch a loud movie in a large, comfortable seat.

The Rooftop of Opposite

Large white seabirds
cuddle and coo and softly
sink into their breast feathers
near a rooftop cement chimney—
chief outlet of soul in our age—
part of the engineering, how
the building breathes, how it
sweats and moans with the spliff
inhalations of its young renters huddled
around the one plastic chair on the balcony
coughing—and farther out
the ships and cranes, the means
of delivery and the tension of economic
and social relations in the shrieking
jaded sirens of 3 a.m. down on Esplanade.

But wait, I get ahead of myself.
It's a nice evening. Still light and bright
at 6:30 just beyond the equinox. Just for laughs
my pink hibiscus aims her orange tongue
at the traffic roar, the heavy commerce on the water.

Wish

Tall girl on Grant Street
in tall boots with naked thighs
turned out like wing bones

amid the goings-on & the traffic
the pedestrian light repetitious
walk don't walk walk don't walk

as I try to be on time
for my 4:30 appointment

comb in hand the stylist explains the cowlick
makes a whirlpool upon the skull,
skyll, schooner, or boat of the soul

I'll inhabit some day, shorn and bare,
aghast under the coffin lid

wishing I'd bought those brown Prada shoes
with the green and red leaves appliquéd

we saw in the window at the casino
in Melbourne beside the River Yarra.

Oh, Hello Count, How Are You, Do Come In

The time and the car have to go. The light has to fall
in a beam from a cloud. The pebbles will rankle.
A stone is a mountain, a mountain a stone.
Sand is carted away. Ants cart a corpse. The hourglass
of their home is a sand volcano. Cobwebs
make hankies upon the shrubbery. The clothes
line sagging with pyjamas under the mad extravagance
of a high double rainbow, now in the photo album.
Is it mica and marble that streak the granite? The Count
loves Gertrude but Gertrude loves Tim. Is it true
we desire desire? Alas
we are the Count, ever hopeful at the door
of immortality like car bombers. I think I ruined those roses,
the ones the deer didn't eat. Sway of tall trees nevertheless
at the edges of the yard each and every
exploding autumn.

Happy Hour

it's always time to do something else
and what's the yardarm the sun should
come over the top of on his round

and the lumpy burn-scarred hills void
of whatever

Eclipse of the Sun

We mustn't kill that vast
old apricot tree with our kindness.
Neglected all these years and now
the sprinkler waves wide plumes
back & forth over the hunched-up tree
festooned with hard little green brats,
surely not all of them her own.

A small paradise even so. They hang from
her limbs in clumps and array. Thunder
roughs up the hills, the sprinkler plumes waver,
the fruit is an ancient offering to strangers
at your door having rambled along the highways
and byways of life.

Apricot-fed strangers with whom you could
quite comfortably witness an eclipse of the sun
without worrying too much they might kill you
or your cutest goat.

Skylarks?

Through the blue
recycling bags you can see the news
of yesterday, the smeared faces,
juice boxes, sheets of instructions.
Omens of a map of increasing
wateriness: the soul, according
to Heraclitus, should not be
moist (a sign of drunkenness)
but rather,
dry. Down in the valley
sirens make a racket.
Now what? Some calamity & calamity
is really spelled *c-l-i-m-a-t-e*.
The thing the guys who know
are really sweating about. The thing
everybody knows unto the very ants
and skylarks.

How to Stay Sane

Despite all that's wrong
    I'd like to go for a walk someday
        among the pearls and carriages
merriment and weather

untoward anything

you talk about volition and overcoming
    I, margarine
        in the aisles of hope
in butter-coloured tubs and pots

geraniums
    mystical, alone and latent
        in the sheds of winter, winter's
shelter, they are

a shade of pink nail polish
    from this season's Greek Collection
        (last year's British Collection
was darker, verging on plaid)

I for one am glad of these mood-lifting changes!

from another yummy shop
    many tasteful items
        carefully tableau'd

luggage and overcoats, mug sets
    at the Great Canadian Superstore
        at Costco

she exclaimed, "I'm here all the time!"
and had just finished writing the real estate exam.
Wow I think yet aver

too much paperwork.
Help yourself is my motto
when it comes to stuff sitting around

like the bags purple in the freezer with last summer's berries.

Not to mention miracles in maroon leather
to be found at Zambesi's
a world away in Wellington

maroon and pumpkin, a different and distant place
from office hours with monitor, minotaur

squatted centre stage
concealing Zambesi cookies.
A three-ring binder on my lap.

Going over a story.
The student is large in the room.
The banners of May yell.

Nameless Dread

A sickened feeling to the right of the heart:
Could it be the news?

Could it be old habits of
let's face it,
repression? How else
get along.

To succumb would be worse
or worse, more telling. One
carries on but without it
being particularly heroic, cf. Beckett,
one
drives the car.

And picks up the groceries
and the dry cleaning. A bunch
of leeks, huge in the bag.

Then to work.
Boot up the computer
and listen to the phone message
from the student with strep throat.

Time passes this way
and then the day. One discusses
naturalism and turns on
the overhead projector

By 4:30 restless, by 5:00
they wish to be detained
by my blabbing no longer. The bus
is waiting, doors swagged open,
driver screwing his smoke out with a toe.

Pine Boughs

top of pine tree bent sideways
like a microphone to the real

what it thinks, okay with us
we're just listening

to the lines and the curves

the woman with prairie behind
or many old loves, a

plain of grass a grass
of prairie plain
as an attitude

whose mist she must
breathe, like in

my dream going down the hall
to Rae's office

with a swelling of cancer
in my right breast near the nipple

in the dream mind you
and I felt all sad and poignant

and different
from the living

a difference I enjoyed for its
brevity and intensity

not that anyone knew
or that the corner office
with the pine boughs out the window
could ever be mine

The Day Lady Di Died

We'd spent the weekend among the tents
and booths at Bumbershoot, then wound back down
through tents and booths deserted as Araby
to the Monorail station.

Lady Di, Lady Di we heard up and down
the aisles—that's what they called her,
Lady Di. A car crash. It was
unbelievable. You're kidding, we said.

But on the hotel-room TV there it was:
the solemn commentator, the closed-off tunnel,
the wreckage. I started feeling homesick &
wanted to hear her properly called Diana
Princess of Wales and that sort of thing,
watch her step out of limousines
in moon-coloured evening gowns,
comfort the sick.

We didn't like being so far away from her style
& her death & hastened to the border
first thing in the morning.

Please Note

The very well-designed magpie,
Schiaparellis of the sky.

It's the teal blue that amazes,
that hat.

February Morning, North Vancouver

Icy parking lot but only on the shady side.
The other smokes with rising steam in sunshine.

It rises also from the blackberry vines reaching
every direction along the path panting
for space, light, spaces pale and creamy
where a blond holds up a garment
from Barney's on a hanger.

Arched cobras of last year's newborn ferns
& slight undressed crocuses huddle in a bunch by the fence.

Legion are the myths of springtime, more
legion myths of springtime's cusp with winter.

Going to Skidegate

I take my homunculus and my purse
        Across the busy parking lot on a hot day
                To the Pharmasave where it is also busy.

People waiting for the blood pressure monitor.
        People picking and choosing their Scratch-and-Wins.
                People with Mars bars and aspirins—

That was the lady behind me. I had a glossy uplifting
        Magazine and a jar of night cream
                And a pair of warm soft socks

So my homunculus would be comforted while the ferry heaved
        And bucked across the Hecate Strait
                And we'd have Mars bars to eat

And magazines to trade
        Once we got to Skidegate.

Birthday Poem

What I do is I make gleam
that which already gleams enough.

When Imagism school's out,
when whatever school is out,
then

I have a smoke and drive
my convertible around
with no one in it.

Why is the sky so blue
in Okanagan Falls?
For that matter,
where is George Bowering,
is his cabriolet
still swerving around run-over
rattlers on MacLean Creek Road?

What about the tall mauve cliff
with black bulls on top
I contemplate out the window
of Our Lady of Lourdes on Sunday mornings?

I'm telling you something
still pushes that mop around
though school's been out
a long long time.

Romantic Poem

The heart, an old city
     — how old?
          Petra. Okay, Paris. More

Magnificent than this old
     getting by,
          older than the old city

the heart is.
     Oh heart
          clutched at when told a sweet story

such as
     the road which was not
          quite the road not taken

but the road
     deferred, possibly
          relinquished.

Yet nonetheless leading to Rome,
     that old city,
          that old pigsty
               of the heart.

How Post-911 The Mystery of Love Became
The Mysterious Mr. Love

Crows pecking around. Cars off in the distance
passing each other peacefully. Like a long day.
Putting on the oven and then changing your mind,
& turning it off again. It's been too long a day.
She wonders where the man with the briefcase went.

There's the house. A detached garage.
A chicken coop. The barn, now used to store
aviation equipment. Like about ten movies
she's a woman alone in a housedress flapping
out rag rugs on the front porch. A car goes by,
slows down. A car from the city.

Crows peck at the wee debris fallen from the rugs.
A cloud covers the sun. The well-scrubbed white
enamel stove an electrical splendour. Inside her head
words collide and slide along each other. How hard
some people find the word "tongue" is to spell:
tounge, tonuge, tong. What she finds hard
is collecting the rent from the guy who's
storing his old cropduster in the barn: the barn,
a kind of cathedral. Did she imagine it, or
did that car from the city seem to be looking for something?

A shiver climbs down from the telephone poles.
A car door shuts firmly, then clomp of expensive city shoes
up the porch steps. Knock-knock-knock lightly, politely.
Excuse me, ma'am, could I have a word with you?
His face behind the screen door smooth and handsome,
his hair is grey and so is his moustache. Beside his right ear
he displays a card with his face on it: Mr. Love.

Come in, Mr. Love, she says. He does. What can she do for him?
He commences asking about who she rents the barn out to. Oh him,
she says. Every month it seems he has a new address,
it's hard chasing down the rent. Mr. Love writes this down
then asks if he can go see the barn. She watches him walk
down the rutted path with his briefcase, a suave good-looking fellow,
the mysterious Mr. Love, stepping around puddles.

On a Rainy Night

The storekeeper comes out
sleepy-looking, interrupted—his shop
low on inventory, more a domicile, smells
of a small supper, a murmur
behind the door-curtain.

I pay for my Sweet Marie.

The storekeeper's eager to return
to his divine literature.
He'll twirl a stick of incense to rinse
the yipping and howling of sirens,
the racks of demoralized candy.

Looped in frangipani & moonlight
the storekeeper and I might have been lovers,
avatars, in another life.

We'd sip at the nectar of truth
and hold ourselves in high esteem.

Milking the spiritual wounds of the West
we'd count up our Rolls Royces,
laugh heartily when asked a question
about the meaning of life
or the meaning of death

and even so
do far less harm
than the Western pine beetle
or fish farms.

Bike Ride to the Rib House

Suddenly through trees ahead
a gleam of blue, the lake!

Nope. A blue tin roof.

Actually,
a blue awning.

Actually the blue and white striped
awning over the back patio
of the Creekside Pub and Rib House—
domicile and breathing cage

of a heart & mind
that saw a gleam and thought, Oh look!
The lake!

Summer Twilight

sunset stripes
azure, peach, crimson, inky blue

twinkling city, movement
of car lights over the floating
bridge, a loner cloud

over closer hills
shaped like the large
crimson lips of wax

we'd buy at the corner store
after school, place them over our own
then bite down and glug

the sweet syrup inside — but this mouth-
shaped cloud is gone now,
broken up,

a wisp, that's about it, that's about all
that's left of our sweet sweet lips.

Nowadays

They made themselves sick arranging for even more credit.
        Things came up on the screen in throbbing turquoise:
                The liquor store purchases. The injured dog.

The new house (a gleam in daddy's eye),
        The warmer weather and the planting of rosemary
           And chives.

They were customers with a bit of a problem —
        Clients, rather. Gold, blue, and platinum
           Their cards throbbed in slots.

How long does "nowadays" last anyway?
        Since the mid-eighties, mid-nineties.

Since Mulroney anyway. They couldn't remember a time
        When the magazines were different
           Or when people weren't so high-strung & managed.

Christmas in Alice Springs

In Melbourne we walked by the water. We stopped for coffee
and as usual other people were there, strangers
speaking Greek. Then we went to Uluru
on a bus through the Outback, hours on end, red sand,
the oldest riverbeds on the planet.

It was Christmas time in Alice Springs. Office functions
tinkled and laughed, kids splashed in Enviro-
suits, poison toads dozed
under a creepy little footbridge and galahs
sailed pink and white as soft cloths through
the air. Aboriginals were partying in the park,
we felt boring, uptight, and white when they passed
barefoot ignoring the sidewalk's direction while Santa Claus
and three tall green elves drove slowly
past sacred sites in the fire engine.

Prologue

I noticed everything—
its transients finding a dime,
its gorgeous detail.

Yet feel remiss
in the quality of my general
attention. The trifling,
the nonsensical
had a short day, relatively
speaking, relative to history.

Someone should write an important poem.

Oh, Danny Boy

First it was really nice out,
a blue September morning.

By one in the afternoon, grey.

By three rain and by now—
late, late in the age of the galaxy—
a thick mist envelops the lights
across the inlet—lights presiding
over who knows what sorts of imports
and exports.

The past has a good laugh.
It sounds like clarinets.

Sidekicks

Sidekicks are a type of lover because
they never let up being attentive.

Bounding across the room to light your cigarette.
Pulling you in under their coat when it rains.

Making lame jokes as you lie
half conscious in a hospital bed,
tubes everywhere. And later on,

Nudging and jostling good-naturedly
as you try your first wobbly steps
out of the wheelchair.

Once fully recovered you both go
honking across an estuary
toward the setting sun in the big semitrailer
you both took lessons at night school to drive.

In the dashboard light of Art Bell's *Coast to Coast*
you tell a ghost story and he makes the sound effects
and up in the sky are flying saucers.

You are abducted by aliens from outer space
who remove the steel pin from your hip and the silver hoop
from your sidekick's left earlobe.

Later on you'll try to remember if it really happened,
or whether you just got carried away
by the long dark road and the twin miracles of each other
& the radio.

Scenes from the Missing Picture

Funny, I hadn't even noticed it was gone.
Then Alice was over—she'd come on her bike,
shaking her blond hair out from the helmet,
pulling the material we'd contracted for
out of her messenger bag. "Here it is," she
said, placing the envelope on the cluttered
kitchen counter—cluttered as only the life
of a flame-haired divorcée could be—kids,
booze, boyfriends, you name it, social workers

Nosing around, late car payments—I lit up
a Parliament (Alice doesn't smoke) and said,
"So, how's it going, kid?" I thought we'd
catch up a bit before getting to the heart
of the matter. Alice didn't want a Cuba Libre
either, she wanted to get back to her apartment
and start working on her new film noir. In
the film she stars as a scuba diver and detective
called Nora Maple. In murky Vancouver inlets

At the edge of night she gets into her wetsuit,
puts on her mask after spitting into the visor, attaches
the hose and jumps feet first off an idling speedboat.
Cement blocks the size of Italians,
rusted-out cars, octopi, cat-clawed sofas all
heaving around in the weedy current—it was some scene
down there all right. Your average tourist snapping
the sunset that flamed over the greasy pink surface
could have no idea what lies beneath.

As a bit of a connoisseur of psychoanalysis
I could relate to Alice's project. I realized
that the unconscious in this post-Freudian
context was a discredited concept, that our best hope
would be to overturn the stack of superego, ego, id,
and put desire back on top—top and centre,
the smartest poodle in the dog and pony show,
both paws raised and a cute little hat on,
the horse bounding round and round the ring.

Alice agreed. She drank a glass of water
and looked around. "Hey," she said. "What happened
to the painting that used to be over there?" She indicated
a large empty space with a nail hole at the top.
I squinted my eyes and puzzled at the wall. We
both remembered at once: "The Great Outdoors"!
In the painting, a man in a canoe paddles away from the
viewer. Large mountains tipped with pinkish peaks
loom around the lone canoeist, lost among loons.

Could someone have purloined "The Great Outdoors"
while I was busy spanking some executive or trying to get
one of the kids to bed? Some thief with gloves on?
Maybe the man in the canoe was a self-portrait
of the thief bidding farewell to the viewer
as he skipped out of the country with a bag of emeralds
worth millions on the black market of blond-seduction,
blond-amelioration, blond-appeasement.

The emeralds matched her eyes. Her nails matched the skies.
Her skirt matched her stilettos and her slip matched her
thong. She was in short a real siren. She'd never be trying
to make ends meet in a lousy condo on the East Side.
Her chinchilla coat she'd lay aside on an armchair at the Wedgewood
and four waiters would be there pronto with order pads
at the ready. It was obvious "The Great Outdoors" was part
of a world of crime and deception of gasping proportions.
Who knew what terrible deals were being made at knifepoint

On an idling speedboat anchored in Horseshoe Bay? "The
Great Outdoors" was just a pawn in a much larger grab for
hydro and hegemony, and it wasn't just about forests.
It was water, it was oil, it was natural gas, it was moose
heads over filmstar fireplaces in Wyoming. Whole rivers
could be diverted to squeeze themselves over dams
so teenagers could download porn off the net. As Alice
and I sat there contemplating the theft of "The Great Outdoors"
we felt like question and exclamation marks respectively.

With a sign bordering on panic, then sadness, then acceptance,
then closure, Alice put her head back in her helmet and
prepared to get back on her bike. One of the kids was crying
so I had to go anyway. Later that evening, looking at the blank wall
and wondering where "The Great Outdoors" had gone, I
glanced at the clutter on the counter and noticed a book
by Nora Maple called *The Mirror Murders*. Was it the clue
to the mystery? I'll bet Nora sees things on a regular basis
that would give H.P. Lovecraft the creeps. Meanwhile

Disposing of "The Great Outdoors" would be no piece of cake.
I felt kind of sorry for the art thief with that
in the back seat trying to be inconspicuous. In the rear
view mirror the canoeist held his paddle on the opposite
side, and the pinkish glow in the sky was that of morn
not eventide. A brownish tinge on shore was proving to be
a rogue moose in heat. "The Great Outdoors" was becoming
a case only Nora Maple could solve.

The phone was already ringing at Alice's house as the
sheepish thief wiped his brow, too frightened now
even to glance into the back seat where "The Great Outdoors"
stood propped, shining, immense, and fragrant — or
was it the cedar-scented bright green
tree shape dangling over the dashboard?

Again

fried and dry
after April's appointment
to go blond

I return
to be dark again

yet
still myself with
mysterious pathways

leading here and
there, over mountain,
down dell, etc.

to times then
in photos
and memory of

the awful deadness
summers could be
upstairs writing

worlds unravelling
unkindly but
at the time felt
necessary

there was so much
left

and still is
though telescoped
somewhat so

one looks out
over the territory
hopefully, with a smile
in your heart

toward
something less crowded
with figures dancing

perhaps or kissing
for the first time
& there you go

again

Lunch

The tomato like a crying child bride was brutally
wed to a tuna. And under plastic
grew very round in the innocent Arctic
while nearby giant icebergs calved. Then
cold, cold upon my sandwich lay
in fishy icy slices. The meat was from the deli.
"Meat" what a word. And the lettuce
sopping purply edges out the sides, thin
clingy plastic bag left near the sink
narrow and all sucked in. Is this
a lunch for the king I really am?
Tetley tea? Standing at
the sliding doors of summer
watching the dogs chase each other round
and round the cherry tree?

THE FIRE

Mars glared
in the firmament
among the shooting stars
the orange moons

mornings cloaked
in terracotta
smoke, yellow pears
pendant in orchards

a fallen, roasted
aspen leaf
Etruscan artefact

among the tongs
and tines of suppertimes

Airplanes lumber
upward, unfold white silk sheets
of lake upon the woods

while the Armed Forces
unpack gear and smooth cots
in tidy tents in city parks

Gloom the breathing element
deposits a half-consumed *Time*
magazine on a parked car
at the mall

and scorched pages
from a first-aid manual: a victim
choking, a victim grasping

at straws, the weather
forecast, the percentage
chance of rain—this means

houses must be burning!

though the fire makes its
own weather anyway

ferocious wind storms

(her hair she demonstrated later
flew straight out in one direction
then suddenly equally straight out in the other direction
as she stood in the yard

and a walloping sound, otherwise
eerie quiet)

they left on bicycles fearing traffic panic

but everyone did go orderly
if terrified and if two followed
fanatic the other's tail-lights all the way
to Starbucks speaking white-faced
into cell phones in the parking lot

I want the house clean
for the fire: to the greater
scourging I offer the lesser.

Windex, floor mop,
sink stopper polished with Vim,
the whole nine yards,
the whole ball of wax.

Last week we'd twirled
Mars to clarity inside
binoculars, discussed
its proximity, its palpable
redness. The likelihood
of "life," what, some weird-
looking worm or germ.

And this morning
the vacuum cleaner is travelling
along behind. I apologize

to a pillow, I can't take you
dear, like throwing a maiden
off a cliff, well, not quite

but the sense of propitiation
was there: Fire, here is a clean floor.
Fire, here is an innocent cushion.

A half moon wears out the night sky,
buttonhole of a jean jacket
worried to thinness
while Mars
lounges among his rights

his stogie—a burning pine forest—
held out at arm's length in order to hear better
the appeals of the widows

My arms feel unattached and threading
even the largest needle
I tremble and miss the eye.

The fallen-off button on a folded towel
near the iron in the quietness
of another house itself
now hazed with smoke.

In the haste to pack, the button
had twirled and flipped, darkness
was about to fall

I bought flashlights
and a round case of needles
as if it were an ordinary errand

helicopters above the roof
sound like something being ground

on my lap the legs and arms
of the garment needing a button

The thread moves to the right
or to the left like a barker's booth
at the circus where you throw softballs
at the passing ducks, it looks so easy

and you really want to win the large pink jaguar

Go ahead fire.
Dot with embers the patios
of citizens trying to dine *al fresco*

aim flame-throwers
at the forest service, the army,
the navy for that matter, who also came
to help

the exhausted and the hold-outs, make
them give up

fall ravenous upon a canyon, reveal
its smoking naked contours

imbue with your stink the fur of the cat

extinguish dwelling-places

just go ahead, you
and your nasty little freaky friend
the wind

Special effects ordered up by Mars
who sits by the pool with maidens either side
buffing his nails in bikinis

we'll do the rooflines aglow
he tells a sycophant with an iPod
we'll do the totally vaporized

We shouldn't be living here
anyway. At night
coyotes howl with laughter
and desire. Mars
is more human.

His attributes ours, his
accoutrements also:
      pool
      chariot
      barbecue
      wrath

My woods are charred
bituminous

black bark bleeds
red resin plasma

between the standing
broiled branchless poles

new unwelcome views of the lake

and of shocked humps of hills
self-conscious and sad, evicted

from their leafy life

naked rock, empty scorched treetops

where for weeks no bird had
or now would

ever sing

And now once more
the wind is blowing
and the fire surges
upon the town
and the countryside

the dear historic

what was lovely

the firs and the pines, etc.

the brown rabbit hopping

the canyon road to the railway trestles
where we took our brother and our mother
on a Sunday or a Wednesday
with its tall ears standing up

I would comfort if I could
but would have to wrestle it down

and feel its scared heart pounding

A stubble of blackened shards
where magpies fly, try
to settle—in autumn light

pine sap looks blue
against bark's carbonic crust

and a spray of brown needles
on the forest floor we pretend

are a carpet of grasses
and not a scorch of tears

upon the miles of roots that smoulder
still in molten maze

where a bluish haze appears to mark

the transit of ghosts and giants
who left an arsonist's hoard heaped

extinct matchsticks leaning
tip to tip

WEEPING WILLOW

1.

Willow tree in winter,
skiff of snow on a wooden bench
placed thoughtful beneath
her boughs —

she'd had wing chairs
specially upholstered —

conversations' nexus —

two of them, the two of us,
our two cigarettes and another

voice going round on the record player
or emanating from a book

swish of traffic outside, her frequent
use of the word *absolutely*

2.

Down Larch St. to suppertime.

Angela'd had another dream
in which a school of fish . . .

& how she should have run off
with the visiting professor . . .

Dear reader,
shouldn't we all have run off with someone.

At any rate
we'd talked for hours at the kitchen table,
Angela dispensing Sweet 'n Low
into her coffee as windows darkened
and it was time to go so

I put on my coat and drove
down the hill in the Honda

many autumns back then

3.

Weeping willow's lanky tresses
hide a bower, an ear

here, the long grass sere in autumn
reminds me of her yellow hair

long and swinging, sleek
when she searched for a lighter—

George you fucking asshole she would say
in the kitchen in her beautiful coat

4.

Scuffed up our new boots in Seattle parking lots,
wore them home across the border.

Salespeople at Nordstrom's back and forth like a crazy-dame movie
with stacks of shoeboxes tottering. Always it seemed

she was at the bank, moving accounts around,
piling up interest —

Furniture arrived in truckloads, a fountain
splashed 'neath newly-installed
Moorish mullioned windows beyond which
a lime-tree bower
her prison —

or so we joked and cackled.

5.

A plain white room the last
of the renovations, protestant
and Northern, where she spoke with Finnish
relatives not long before she died. Down the hall ornate
birds and vines clambered rococo over walls and ceilings

where once she'd presided
over ten million calorie dinner parties—

Oysters Rockefeller, Angel-Tit pie,
& much between that was
silky and rich

6.

In memory murmurs, deep
Venusian glow of her topaz ring.

She was a James Bond type of woman,
with green eyes.

In our houses reviewing
some recent event uneventful really
to the naked eye. Golden green the topaz
slips sideways on her paperwhite finger,
hand to mouth, hand to mouth, it was
the *J'accuse* of the student questionnaires —

That Thomas Hardy was way too hard.
That she'd be late, or bring a muffin,
or go on and on.

7.

We drank Piesporter, ate oysters raw &
Rockefeller. Silk slid around in shopping bags.
I went to her dentist—the very one on call
whenever the Queen came to town

and soon seed catalogues were stacked
on the table & she was happy in the garden,
her new inamoratae roots and branches, rare

or uncommon and common as well,
beloved, poetry a balustrade
in all the rooms indoors and out

8.

Arrayed in the plentiful hues
of the fashion then
and also now but then
we seldom took a walk

& the longer it's been
the younger we become

the two of us in a kitchen
our children in the next room
playing and murmuring

"primitive philosophers"
she would say

tears welling

9.

As she lay dying amid the willow branches
a gardener pruned a Moorish vista from a row of trees

and the church across the street gonged with weddings
and with funerals, or the ordinary Sundays with the old
faithful getting out of cars and opening umbrellas

and wings of angels began to fill the room
and crowd out the physiology,
the husband, the daughter

the pile of mysteries on the bed.

10.

Reading a novel called *Being Dead*
and how windy and cold it is
in the everlasting hills.

I wish Angela were here.

We would talk and what we
talked about would knit together
a garment

in the willow bower where she sheltered
her unmendable body

11.

Willow tree—fortress
and boudoir, rehab
of the mind-body split

Angela, I say,
I can't write love poems.

That's alright, she says.

12.

Thinking pours from her hair,
head-to-toe silk on the way to the car,
fresh cigarette in ivory holder
clenched to one side
as she reached back into coat arms—

perfume floating, rainy day, time to go

ACKNOWLEDGEMENTS

Thanks to The Canada Council; to Jenny Penberthy, who read an early version of the manuscript; Robert Bringhurst, whose translations of Haida epic poetry, *A Story as Sharp as a Knife*, inspired the cadences of "The Good Bacteria" sequence; Peter and Meredith Quartermain for publishing "Weeping Willow" as a Nomados chapbook; Rachel Zolf, poetry editor of *The Walrus*, for publishing a version of "Oh, Hello Count, How Are You, Do Come In" in the December 2005 issue; Jeremy Dodds for publishing versions of poems from this book in *The Third Floor Lounge*; Joan Goodman, who met me in Woodward, PA for Frances Boldereff's funeral and with whom I visited Jerry Geiger in Aaronsburg; Alice Tepexcuintle; and to Paul Mier, my husband. And thanks to Ken Babstock, for his astute and helpful editorial advice.

This book is dedicated to Lina Delano, artist and friend, who speaks the line "Caio, Marcello, com estai?," and others, in Federico Fellini's film, *La Dolce Vita*.

PHOTO: PAUL MIER

ABOUT THE AUTHOR

Sharon Thesen has published seven books of poetry. Her work has twice been shortlisted for the Governor General's Award for Poetry. Her last book with Anansi, *A Pair of Scissors*, won the prestigious Pat Lowther Memorial Award. Sharon Thesen was born in Tisdale, Saskatchewan, and she now lives in Vancouver, British Columbia.